The Red Coat

Jane Ellen Glasser

*For Susan & Malcolm —
With love,
Jane
1-18-2013*

FUTURECYCLE PRESS

Mineral Bluff, Georgia

Published by FutureCycle Press
Mineral Bluff, Georgia, USA

ISBN 978-1-938853-12-8

Contents

I

II

III

IV

V

VI

I

The Long Life

There is no other that you are waiting for.
Everything you need is within your reach.
When the towhee sings his name in the maple tree
outside your window, sing back your name.
The wind will carry it downriver

to distant estuaries. Think of how hard
you have had to work to get to this moment,
how many soles you have discarded
along the way, how many moons have waned

like shuttered lanterns. Now you are light inside.
Now you have cast off parents, children,
a house, expectations, demands, politics.
You have earned the right to be self-ish.

Be like the heron who stands on the glistening
shoreline tucked into her wings.
Roam the countries in the two continents
inside your head. Speak to the natives,
all those people you have been and are.

All you have to do is listen.

How to Start a Day

Begin by letting go of the hem
of your dream. Let it slip
backwards into a black lake
as you greet the dawn. Be thankful
for small aches. You have survived

night's heavy arms to wash yesterday
from your face. Begin to create
the opus of a new day. Look out
from a kitchen window as you savor
a first cup of coffee. House wrens

flap at the feeder. A squirrel
dances osiers so that the willow
shakes with laughter. Be thankful
for the small favors of sunlight
walking across the lawn, a cabbage

butterfly teasing the azaleas,
the pink rain of cherry blossoms.
Even the neighbor's dog barking
ducks from his yard is sacred.
Open to morning's hymns:

the big mouth of the garbage truck,
the mockingbird's purloined songs,
chatter on the corner waiting
for the yellow school bus. The engine
of the day purrs in your throat

as you dress. Sweep your calendar
clean of doctor appointments,
chores. The vacuum and the duster
can wait. Let the day surprise you.
Be thankful to be who you are.

A Brief Existential Rumination

Old Maid was a child's game
I grew into. I believed once

in the gibberish of a rose.
I've buried a husband and three

lovers in memory's boneyard,
getting by on a daughter's handouts

and a diet of poems.
Now touch is my beggar's cup.

I've locked away two rabbis
in reason's attic.

Like the wayside cornflower
that pushes up in gravel,

I'm an outsider. There's no one
to betray my secrets

or wound me with a
sister's tongue. To ease my load,

I've stowed on Charon's ferry
envy, anger, spite, greed.

A lightweight, I can ride
the wind like seed or scuttle

and hide like a sand crab.
What is my purpose?

What is the purpose of a stone
in a creek's bed, or a weed?

A Reminder to Myself of What I Love

Slipping into an envelope
of clean sheets;
anything that goes
by the name of *comforter*;
dreams that outstay
waking's whiteout;
snake wisdom
in letting go
of the outgrown;
a blank day;
bagels, donuts, anything
that says it's okay
to be empty at its center;
moving out of the penthouse
of my head;
the alchemy of touch;
big weather;
twilight's reprieve;
stargazer-breath;
the little engine
of morning coffee;
cappuccino jelly beans;
by the roadside,
a golden spill of daffodils;
a tree's root and reach;
a mountain cabin beside
a singing creek;
the meditation of
an egret's ellipse;
good manners;
blue cheese;
a squall's heavy drapery
sweeping toward shore;
bursting from a tree,
a ragged scarf
of blackbirds.

Truths I Tell Myself

Meaning has to be made,
like Hardy's biscuits,
fresh every morning.

To avoid arrogance,
cultivate a few bad habits
but don't take pride in them.

Aloneness is a temple;
loneliness, its desecration.

No two people
speak the same language.

If nothing exists
to pull you into the future,
you are already dead.

Devote your days
to searching for answers.

There are no answers.

A Daily Practice: From *The Book of Survival*

You return home after a busy day.
Slowly the traffic dissolves
in a pool of silence. Bar the door
to the room you create for yourself.

A life without privacy is a sideshow,
a beggar's cup. Undress. Take off
what the morning put on: shoes,
a watch, a face of expectation.

Take off what the day put on,
its heavy coat of hours. Swing open
the gates of the prison house:
release guilt, fear, hunger, ambition.

The one who leaves crying
Me! Me!, pardon her too.
Stretch. Feel each cell breathe.
Sit down. Put your feet up. Listen

for the hosannas of toes and fingers
freed from indentured service.
One by one, give your organs
away. Lay the tongue in its crib.

Close your eyes as images swim past:
tetras, angels, bottom-feeders.
Net nothing. Be the nothing
of yogis and madmen. In time,

the world will return. In time,
you will return, mind and body
refreshed, ready to take on
the difficult work of living.

II

Grandpa's Tulips

Every fall Grandpa crippled himself
digging holes, six rows across,
from Old Nyack Turnpike
to his hold-everything garage.

By April the drive up to his house
burst into every color in my crayon box.
I liked the parrots best, a tropical blend
of oranges, reds, greens, the glossy petals

edged like a lady's slip. His daughters,
Mother and three aunts, would swoop in
from the city with huge buckets.
I'd watch them, bending in their bright

spring dresses, brushing their hair back,
cursing their heels sinking into the dirt.
While Grandpa watched wrestling on TV,
in an hour the long bed was stripped.

I rode home in a Cadillac packed with tulips.
I could hardly breathe.

Grandma Mamie's Kitchen

She used to live in the kitchen
that smelled of Limburger cheese
and fried onions, Grandpa's favorites.

Are you hungry, maidela?—her litany
to me when I came to visit. Morning to
night she'd cook and bake love up.

Passover, she made family of anyone
left at home without a seder.
Everything she made from scratch.
Everyone cried over her horseradish.

She measured by feel, a bissel this,
a bissel that. When her mind went bad
as soft fruit, when the family lost,

in a slow erasure, her sweet-and-sour
cabbage, potato kugel, kreplach,
she'd sit in her wheelchair by the TV

watching wrestling and westerns
with Grandpa. He'd sit beside her
silence and hold her hand.
She'd look at him, reaching for a

name. The nurse fed her peptic foods
from the cabinet. Grandma's hands
kneaded the blanket in her lap.

Dance Lessons

Because her husband was sent to jail,
Maury Baker's mother taught ballroom dancing.
Friday nights I'd put on my good dress
and black patent Mary Jane's. The tallest

in an odd number, I was partnered
with Mrs. Baker while the other girls
thrilled to a boy's hand along their waist.

Held close in a box step, her breasts
against my cheek, my left arm
couldn't reach her shoulder. I wondered

what Mr. Baker did to be locked away.
Did he murder someone or place his hands
where they didn't belong on little girls?

While Mrs. Baker counted out dance steps
to love songs on a Victrola, we circled
the floor. *Don't look at your feet,*
she'd chide us, holding her head up high.

What His Gift of Flowers Said

—for Hieu Tran

Flowers at my door just now—
purple-tinged white lilies
for old "teachah."

How many years ago was it?
The course was composition.

His native tongue was America's
wound; his blood, a jungle of America's
lost boys.

He never raised his hand.
He never raised his head.
He never raised his pen.

Afternoons he'd return to my classroom.
Some days he was a distant place,
a little hut of silence.
Some days he talked
about his family—the white ghost
of his father, his good-in-English
baby sister, his girlfriend
whose parents demanded for their daughter
a bright scholar.

I'd sit across from him and listen
as his words spilled out
like sea pearls, irregular shapes
I worked to smooth and string together.

What is knowing
but patience and translation
at a border where two bodies,
those foreign countries, meet?

I could not do otherwise.
I failed him.
I never failed him.

Sunday at Stockley Gardens Art Show

From a crooked mouth,
How many times must I tell
you...! The boy stood frozen
in a growing puddle of shame

as the woman turned to tell
the back of one who could not face
what had become his shame.
Like a dog, the man kicked up dirt

in this public place of turned faces
milling about like city park birds.
The boy disappeared behind dirt-
stained fingers, but in just seconds

his hands flew, startled birds,
to tangle in his sister's hair.
He must have been the second,
a darkling fallen between

sweet and sweeter, his fair-haired
and fair-skinned sisters, Mother's
darlings. Years ago, something between
husband and wife, some unsaid thing,

had fisted inside the mother's
belly. Booth to booth he raced,
knowing by touch, touching everything—
pottery, paintings, prints—

until the prodded father raced
after him, gripping his son's thin arm
so tight he'd leave his print,
and dragged him toward the car.

The Last Visit

The last passengers were already met
when Father steered her elbow
down the walkway. Frangible,
she shuffled forward.

I watched her grow and shrink
as she approached. Outside
the terminal, she wasted little
time in lighting up, her gold

cigarette holder—the pen
to sign her death. She'd been
sick so long it was like a
tired dress she'd wear forever.

Always Mother was so there
she was not there. At first
she was convenient as a closet,
safe as covers in night's room.

Later, she reined in adolescence
with an electric fence, then
sent me to places on a map
she'd never been.

In letters she never talked
about herself, her illnesses,
her soured marriage.
After my divorce she said,

Who will want you at your age
and with two children?
And then her mouth squeezed
like a tourniquet on silence.

There was nothing special
to remember about the visit.
I must have cooked.

Dad watched TV.
She watched the girls
while I cleaned or ran errands.

And then she was gone.

Woman in ICU

Days when friends come to visit, her husband
fixes her hair, applies makeup. They put on
smiles and press around her bed, touching

her hands, feet, forehead, as if to make this
version of her real. She speaks with her eyes.
I am sick of being sick, they say. Her world

has compressed to a room, a bed, a TV
for the nurses' viewing. On the windowsill,
each week's dozen blood-red roses from

her husband. Love tires her out. Living tires
her out. And yet, what wouldn't she give
to feel rain stippling her skin, to walk the

aisles of a grocery store. After two months
on a ventilator, tube-fed, supine as a dead fish,
she wonders if she'll ever get out. Emptying

light-headed, vertiginous as the zip of a pricked
balloon, might be what dying would feel like.
Or lulled on morphine, easy as slipping a hand

from a glove. Death is the door she could open
(she has this power left) to remove herself
from suffering and loosen into nothingness.

Yet the IVs keep her here, as if tethered
to the ground. And the ventilator that
breathes for her. And fear.

Boardwalk, Hollywood Beach

It's nice to see them
holding hands, the overdressed
old couple, watching youth
blur past on roller blades.

Strolling the boardwalk,
the man still turns to catch
the scantily clad and is wistful
for a moment. His oldest memories
are his truest friends.

Now and then his wife leans closer
to his good ear. They have arrived
at that place where they talk about
everything. Where they have to
talk about everything. What else
could have made them
newlyweds again?

Yesterday the doctor was direct.
There is nothing left to do but
nickel and dime it.

Tonight they would speak
about arrangements. How he was
to go. How she was to live.

This afternoon they have chosen
to let the ocean wash them
clean of fear and sadness
and the grief that anticipates grief.

They weave in and out
of young couples
holding hands, they steer
around bicycles, the ruckus
of racing children,
they inhale smoked meat
pouring from a café.

Terminal

—for Courtney

You need to touch her. You need
to be physical, your hand on bone
at her wrist, the loose sleeve
of her upper arm. When the nurse asks,

she holds up seven fingers and you know
by her pinched face she means ten.
Now, every three hours, she will float
on calm waters, the land a distant blur.

Your father is off in his own country
where God has promised him a miracle.
He speaks to his wife in future tense:
restaurants, movies, a trip. *Terminal—*

the word that broke you open,
as if death were a station for homecoming
after a long voyage. It will fall to you,
daughter, to make arrangements.

Past Midnight

Because his programs were over
and he couldn't sleep,
the man let his dog walk him.

The dog stopped at every tree,
lifting his leg to write his name—
a palimpsest—over another's scent.

The man had lost his first name
with the death of his wife, his friends.
On this clear night of scattering leaves,

he thought of his sons
prospering in distant cities.
Once around the block,

past the yellow moons
of porch lights, past the familiar houses
whose residents kept changing,

the dog returned the man to his house.
As they climbed the splintered steps
the man, an amateur astronomer,

looked up at the constellations,
communities that stayed the same:
Pisces, Scorpius, Sagittarius,

Perseus, Centaurus, Cassiopeia...
He said the names out loud
to hear his own voice.

Dolor of the Abandoned House

My windows watch the street for signs.

I thought, *vacation,* but she's been gone
six months. Orchids scatter
paper ghosts on tabletops.
The stove's mouth, left open,
sighs. Every day it rains

dust. Too old to start over, I worry
about auctions, moving vans,
children screeching, scuffing
my floors as strangers move in.

Would she do this to me?

Who has loved her more?
Not the husband who walked out
on us. Not the daughters
who married faraway cities.

Who knew her better than I did?
My walls have swallowed tears
and laughter. My sofa holds her shape.

I ache for the caress of air as she moves
through rooms, the patter of her feet,
the seasons of her moods.

Late summer and the lawn is wild,
gone to weed. The mailbox yawns
on its post. Camellias litter the front steps
like rusted memories.

Suspended in time, I wait
the way a dog waits, listening
for footsteps, the kiss of her key.

Earhart's Last Poem

One more good flight left, she said.
Then she'd let words take wing,
set free the heart's birds:
falcon, buzzard, starling,

emotions that lived and died
beneath the sun's glow.
*To catch molten moments from
the fire of life* she dared to go,

determined as Icarus,
to write her longest poem
upon the air. July first, calm
weather, a quiet day at home,

her husband George napping
in his easy chair, she flew
around the world she loved
in headline news.

(Italicized lines represent Earhart's words.)

The Millionaire

A woman is scrubbing a pan, still in her
curlers and bathrobe, when the doorbell

that would change her life rings. Caught
in a camera's eye, Sophie stares at a big smile,

an extended hand. She's confused.
She's embarrassed by her appearance.

She's crazy with disbelief. She reaches
for the check and reads. "Arnold!" she screams.

"Arnold, oh my God, Arnold, come quick!"
You know the story. He quits his job

and blows his dough on blackjack
in Atlantic City. Sophie's relatives are

merciless. New homes. New cars. Soon
the couple's broke. The marriage falls apart.

She has a love affair with the butcher.
They get hitched. Every night she cooks

up a feast with red meat from his shop.
For the first time in her life, Sophie

is really happy. As for Arnold, he's content
to get back his old job as janitor at the bank.

Fat Girl

Mornings the bathroom
mirror frowns
at a sideshow.

Who is it that wears
this stranger's body?

I'm a blowfish
of my former self,
a mouth hungry
as a garbage truck.

Whose clothes are these
that don't fit?

There's a wide river
between the banks
of a zipper.
Buttons pop off
like question marks.
Trapped inside
rolling hills,
my bones smother.

At night I dream
of a self thin
as a Brancusi sculpture,
light as the landing
of a *pas de chat.*

There's so much of me
men no longer see me.
Women turn away.
Children stare.

I'm the emptiest
fat girl on the planet.

Blind Girl Talking to a Tree

Rough-skinned, wider
than my arm's embrace,
give me your name
so we can be friends.

I'm told you reach
higher than my house,
your limbs busy with leaves.

Tell me their shape and color
though I will never know color.

You don't have to tell me
about birds that make a home
in your branches.

I know them by their songs.

Tree, tell me what it feels like
to lose something
one leaf at a time.

Then tell me what it's like
when the snow comes
and the flood of darkness comes,
and I'll say, I know, I know.

III

The Imagined Man

I thought of him on my way home
from visiting my daughter in Florida.

Thousands of feet above the coastline,
at sixty-four I decided to play God.

I gave him features, a pastiche of parts
that had attracted me to others.

I dressed him from Saks. To please
my children, I made him Jewish.
I named him *Henry.*

I gave us a history. Recently met,
we frustrated our waiter by kibitzing
for hours before ordering.

We saw each other when we talked.
We let the past be past.

Later, instead of fingering popcorn,
we held hands in the movies.

Teenagers again, we necked
on a bench at the waterfront
under the tipped smile of a moon.

Our bodies vibrated after touch
like tuning forks.

I was about to slip into lingerie
when the plane landed in Norfolk.

What Else But Love

After The Birthday *by Marc Chagall*

What else but love could elevate the heart so?
His green velvet jacket floats above his beloved.
His legs hang loose as clothes on a line.
His torso, cylindrical as a bullet, arcs at the neck
so that, eye to eye, the kiss

that began at the door continues as they move
into the room. She, too, feels light-headed,
the folds of her black dress drawn back
like a wing. One foot is off the floor, the toe
of the other barely grazing the red carpet.
She holds a bouquet of roses like a bride.

The room is spare: a bed, a stool, a table.
On the table, the cake she baked that morning,
pomegranate seeds. Today they will celebrate

his birthday. Defying the laws of nature,
he will never grow older; he will never fall
out of love.

Gardenias

Years ago, when kissing was nourishment,
my lover planted a miniature in my bed.
I'd place the cut flowers in a little vase.
In three days the petals yellowed like ivory.

In six months, he was gone. Everyone said
tempestuous starts end badly. Be wary
of excess. Just one can perfume
an entire room with its heavy scent.

When the plant died, I replaced it
with a standard. Yesterday, as I snipped
a bloom and cupped it to my nose,
my senses raced again. I thought of him.

This man I hardly know. I arranged
gardenias in a bowl and set them on the
coffee table beside a bottle of merlot.
The air was aphrodisiac for wine-laced

talk. I learned about his alcoholic father,
his grandchildren, his divorce. For my
daughter's wedding I wore a gardenia
corsage. The pin struck close to my heart.

All night I was intoxicated by this stranger.
This spring the bush in the side yard is heady
with blooms. I'll keep my senses aroused—
place gardenias in every room.

Contemplating *Lovers in the Red Sky*

"It's always the first time," you like to say
afterwards. From our still-warm bed I stare
at Chagall's lovers afloat on a day
that lasts forever. Impossibly, they share
one body, a sacred knot. He never
leaves for work. She never returns below
to the house in town to cook their dinner.
They never argue. They will never grow
apart from the tedious wash of years.
Bathed in the red glow of an always sun-
set, they suspend transfixed above the fears
that plague the likes of us. Lovemaking done,
we fall to earth. Clocks reclaim the hours.
I worry about dinner. You rise to shower.

Hiking Brokenback Mountain

The trail was narrow. I followed you up Brokenback
Mountain like a stunted shadow. I carried
my field guide for wild flowers, their names—tokens
of their faces: black-eyed Susan, butterfly weed,
foxglove. The path was steep. I had to walk
slowly, catching breath, and fell behind. It took
a while for you to notice. On hikes you never talk.
You lose yourself in the grandeur of where you look;
that day—the sun filtering through the fire
of turned leaves, the outcroppings of limestone
stippling the mountainside, a hawk's sweep. The air
was crisp with frost. I had never felt more alone
than on that mountain. I should have known better.
Nothing would be in bloom in late October.

The Red Kayak

You nosed the red kayak into
the river; we glided blind
through a thick screen of fog.

I was behind you. Your arms
worked while I sat still in the
haze of last night's argument.

You had packed everything
you thought we'd need to return
to the garden: stargazer lilies,

my favorites; scented candles,
our music, wine. I'd packed
lingerie in a suitcase of doubt.

The sun rose, burning off the fog.
I know what I want! you had said.
I stared at the life preserver

on your back. My arms grew
tired, drawing wheels in and out
of the water. The only sound,

a honking trail overhead.
We had used up our voices
exhuming the past.

In the kayak, we were
aimed 90 degrees toward
that thin, black horizon.

Winter Storm

She woke to white fields and a screen of snow
so thick she could barely see the shed.
He had left early. There was another place
to go to once night fell. Tree to tree, a red

cardinal stitched the white air.
The garden that had worked her hands
all spring and summer lay buried. She felt sad
this morning, looking out on so much land

that held nothing. She would always wake
with a cold place beside her in the bed.
He would always return to the house in town
for the children's sake. She had read

the winter storm was coming. She was prepared
to wait it out. The distance between, a backroads
route, would go unplowed for days. She stared
at the dwarf maple, bent low by its heavy load.

The white-roofed feeder swung in the wind
like a ghost's lantern. She told herself it was good
enough that he wanted her. Before he left,
he had chopped and brought in wood.

The Dance

After Dominatrix Embracing her Client *by Diane Arbus*

He holds on as they shift weight
to the slow music. One shadow dances
on the bare wall. Her black hair drapes
to lace stockings. He is naked
except for his socks and shoes,
his eyeglasses pressed to her cheek.
It does not matter that she is half his age.
It does not matter that his penis against
her thighs is a sleeping animal. She is paid
to be whatever he needs her to be.
For one hour this night, they dance.

The Woman and the Beast

After Who Then? *by Donna Iona Drozda*

The woman cannot help herself.
She is pulled toward the beast
the way plants torque toward light.

The beast cannot help himself.
In the clutch of longing
he has traveled the heavens,

howling the sun awake.
For years, she had hunted him
in forests, in jungles, in dreams

of her own flesh. Now,
suspended in cobalt, across stars,
hand to claw they reach.

A Synecdochic Meeting

A brown hat walked into the café.
His cigar made the rounds of tables
until, there, in the back corner,
a hand greeted him. It had been 5 years

since their eyes met. He had married
a desk; she had married a house
with a picket fence. She was still
raven hair and ruby lips. He was still

a moustache and suit. Their plates
cooled as they reminisced. Their heads
communed as if she had no little mouths
waiting at home. "Was there anything else

you wanted?" the white jacket asked.
Her watch sighed. The cigar waved
him away. She lifted the bubbles
of Dom Pérignon and toasted

what might have been. Their hearts
clinked glasses. When the bottle was empty
and the waiter's smile was tipped,
their lips said a long and last goodbye.

Paul Had It Wrong

After Corinthians 1

Love is not patient, not kind. It runs
on four legs like a dog. Arrows tattoo
its heart. Rude, it refuses to come
when called. Promises to be true

write themselves in chalk on rainy days.
Jealousy is its middle name. It boasts.
It begs. It insists on its own ways.
Love has an end but never goes. Ghosts

haunt dreams' corridors, rejoice
at wrongs. Like faith, it is a blind crone.
Like hope, a child with a sugary voice
asks you to bear all things for its own

sake. O, curses of the heart, above
all the greatest of these is love.

IV

The Death of the Poet Li Po

Some say it was the wine. Some say it was love,
the moon smiling up at him from the river.
He was drunk. The boat was tipsy. He stood,
aching to embrace such loveliness forever.

The stars looked on. The lapping waves
were dancing. Leaning out over the gunwale,
he toasted his image which lay now beside
the moon's face and drank again. The sails

billowed and the little craft rocked him forward.
He could not deny himself. He reached and reached
until the river opened its mouth and drank him.
The boat was lost in the blackness. The beach

was miles away. This was Li Po's last line.
Some say it was love. Some say it was the wine.

Exode

*The exit song of the chorus after the last episode
in a Greek tragedy*

Were the gods sleeping when the eagle,
a turtle clutched in his talons,
wafted inland? Steered by hunger,
the yellow eye searched the streets of Gela.

Where were the gods when out for a walk
Aeschylus watched fishing boats
shrink from shore?

The sun was blinding that day.
Here and here: roof tiles, entablature, a statue.
And then mistaking Aeschylus's bald head
for a rock, the eagle let go.

Room 11, Hotel Hellman, Stockholm

In memory of poet Dan Andersson, who died
of accidental asphyxiation 16 September 1920

We sprayed the mattress
and changed the linens.

The man sat writing
at the desk. He hummed
as he wrote, the way men do
when they're lost in work.

He scratched at the red
marks on his chest.

The airless room filled
with the smell of almonds.

Outside the rain
was composing a poem.

We never meant any harm.
We did as we were told.

Sergei Aleksandrovitch Esenin's Last Poem

Here's the night table with its lit candle.
Here the looped rope dangling from a pipe
like a question mark or a hand-held
strap on a crowded bus. I am going on a trip.

Not far away. One step. One small kick,
a little dance and the light goes out.
I am sick of the industry of living, sick
of sleepless nights. Elizaveta, no doubt

true to your word, unopened my poem
written in the wine of my blood
sits in your pocket like a worry stone.
No stitched brow. No flood

of tears. A last breath, the psyche flies.
Goodbye, my friend, goodbye.*

The first line of Esenin's poem

Tour Guide in the Musée du Louvres

After La Grand Odalisque *by Ingres*

It's the torso we see first, its languid,
sweeping curve that lures us in. Let critics
argue the deformation of the arm,
the extra vertebrae, the too small head;
the body's seduction is no less perfect.
The rondure of the breast, the buttocks
are like ripe fruit beckoning to be taken.
Dressed in a jeweled turban and bracelets,
she holds a peacock fan, its many eyes
against her thigh. As if to repeat a theme,
we're next drawn to her gaze—aloof—
as if years of harem life have worn her down.
Imagine holding this pose for hours...
Maybe it's the end of a day and she's masking
a stiff neck, the chill of a drafty studio, hunger,
restlessness. Or perhaps she's just taken
a toke of opium from the hookah by her feet,
withdrawn to a foreign place we cannot reach.

Botero's *The Dancers*

Are they not beautiful to watch?
The obese señora—so light on her feet,
with her left leg raised, the toe
of her right shoe barely grazes the floor.

Dressed in Saturday-night black, solid
as a landmass, the mustachioed señor
grips her mid-back and swirls her
around the small-town dance floor.

The shock of her hair waves like the tail
of a red fox. Her purple dress, sheer
silk, advertises the monuments of her
buttocks. Does it matter that both of them

will likely suffer from diabetes or heart
failure, that the woman's exposed limbs,
as if helium-inflated, appear they would
burst with a pin prick? Thankfully,

the dancers are frozen in the moment
when they're so in step, their bodies meld
as they move in the heat of a tango.
We cannot see the señora's face

that gives her man a cheek, but surely she's
swooning. As for the señor, because he
knows we're witnesses to an unlikely scene,
he looks straight at us and winks.

After *The Loss of Virginity*

In Gauguin's painting, the maiden lies naked,
stretched out on the earth like a corpse.

    Afterward, I covered myself with a white sheet
    as he rose to shower and dress.

She holds a wilted iris in her right hand.
Everything in the canvas is something else.

    We were going to be married that summer.
    Mother had selected daisies for the altar.

Her left hand embraces the evil-eyed fox
who places his paw on her heart.

    My parents were pleased. Following my romance
    with artists—a sensible lawyer.

Her eyes are closed and her feet cross
like Christ's on the crucifix.

    He slipped into business talk. He had maps
    in his shoes, money in his mouth.

The villagers move off to church or to a wedding.
The red fields of Le Pouldu are harvested.

    I dressed while he planned our future:
    where we'd live, what cars we'd drive, our two children.

One cloud in the blue sky, an echo of the maiden's body,
suspends in the heavens like a cry.

Sunday Afternoon on the Island of La Grande Jatte

On a day that will last forever, Parisians are out
in the sunlit park on the banks of the Seine.
Some sit or stand to face the river. Young and
old, *beau monde* and bourgeoisie, nature sustains

them on this radiant afternoon as they gather
on the grass to do nothing. A small dog sprints
in the foreground, in contrast to these bright
figures who seem frozen, shapes that only hint

at people inside. The couple who own the right
side of the canvas puff up as fashion plates.
A coffee cup would balance on Madame's bustle.
Everyone, even those who came with mates,

seems lost in an inner meditation that keeps
them separate—but not lonely. Instead
of men's rowdy calls and children's laughter,
here all is silent, fixed in a sacred creed

of timelessness. Parasols open like flowers.
Trees throw down area rugs of shade
for lounging. No one's reading a book. No one's
holding hands or embracing. No one's laid

out a picnic. Boats on the river go nowhere.
The grass is flat and neat as a tablecloth.
No one litters. Life is orderly and safe.
It's as if Seurat has stopped the world to get off

and land us in a place where all coexist in peace,
where every figure subsists in solitude yet defines
the whole. It confounds modern temperaments,
we who live in desperate and disorderly times.

Le déjeuner sur l'herbe

I'm not embarrassed. No, my fixed stare
suggests only that you're interlopers on the scene.
Oh years ago I could rouse a media storm.
Today my nakedness seems nominal. Clean

country air; a tipped basket of fruit,
a knot of bread; for cloth, the sweet
summer grass—this outing is a holiday from
my cramped flat, heat-swollen city streets.

A friend came with me. By the sun-lit bank
you'll find her, just risen from a bath,
slipping into a white chemise. Surely you've
entered into places like this, where faith

distills your life to one shimmering afternoon
and lets you rest there. But Manet tried
to warn us about opposites. Since you've
stayed, baffled by the canvas, I'll confide

there *is* something indelicate here. Business
suits at a picnic! Our dates refused to remove
their jackets and cravats. One stares off, bored,
into the distance. My suitor in the hat reproves

critics of the latest exhibit at the Salon
des Refusés as if I weren't here. Their
presence makes me more naked than I am.
Visitors to the museum can't help but stare.

V

Laurel Wood Cabin

Set in a cluster of laurels halfway up
Brokenback Mountain, weathered
by fifteen winters of snow, the cabin

is cousin to these woods I walk
to find myself in the metrics of bird song,
the gifts of lilies and lady slippers.

Inside, vaulted ceilings overhang
spare rooms where picture windows
deliver postcards of wilderness.

Yesterday, I watched a doe by the creek
watching me. New on her feet, her legs
splayed out like a busted card table.

This morning on my walk,
I spied a blue jay sounding his name
j-a-a-y from the yellow poplar,

a red spider scribbling his way
along a dirt path, a rabbit sprinting
from the flame azalea. Now dusk,

I sit on the wraparound porch
as trees melt into the greater darkness
and a sawing chirr lifts from the ground.

I tell myself I am a pebble
on the mountain's back,
the moon is a comma on eternity.

Japanese Cherry Blossom

Such abundance of a nothing weight!—
each blossom fully opened yet holding on.
Now a squirrel dances, thin limb to limb,
and the whole tree shivers. And now
a cardinal alights in his swashbuckler's habit
to breakfast on a delicacy. Tomorrow
the wind will begin its scattering work
and it will rain pink petals for a week.
As reverie follows bliss, green will follow pink.
And green can live for months on memory.

After Fire

Above a ruin of trees, crows stream.
There is music in their wings,
a peculiar lilt to their fragmentation
of grief. The moon balances
on a blackened branch where, of late,
an owl sat. Deer have scattered.
Where did the squirrels and voles hide?
Their prints mark the ashen ground
like hieroglyphs. Now the wind comes
to soothe. From nowhere, a cardinal
blazes—a red gash on a black canvas,
so beautiful the stars cry.

A river would never insist

that the life of its banks
bow to its great body
or that the earth yield
to its hunger.

It would never presume
to swallow rocks, trees,
towns, humble stars
or proselytize to fish.

Time has shown it the way
all things follow on their own.
It has no motor;
it goes by letting go

and never stops to question
what greater power pulls it
or what moods its marriage
to the elements will expose.

It gushes, streams, walks
in its sleep, gallops, leaps,
trusting in the alchemy
of moon, tide, weather.

The Egret

You arrive on the river alone, not alone
like a widow or an abandoned house—

more like a hermit content on his mountain
to be partner to the woods.

How slowly, methodically you move
so that beneath the still surface

what blue crabs or silver fish see
is a black reed lifted and lowered like a quill.

Safety, they read as your keen eye
signals the stiletto of your bill.

You are so good at nourishing yourself.
Afterwards, on one leg at the land's end,

you slip into the perfect white ellipse
of a meditation.

Constitutional

As a child, it was my job
to follow our terrier's nose
around the block. Now,

for forty minutes each day,
I walk the old dog
of my bones, a happy vessel

for wind and sun,
lemony scent of magnolias,
confluence of bird song.

A cardinal swoops down
to preen in the rainbow-
spattered spray of a sprinkler.

Two boys in caps, like birds
with their bills on backwards,
blur by on skateboards.

An automobile honks
geese to the side of the road.
I hum as I walk. I am never alone.

My shadow knows when to lead,
when to keep beside me,
when to follow me home.

After Moving from Virginia to Florida

Here where winter
strolls the avenues
in shorts and florid shirts,

hibiscus lick the air
with honeyed tongues
and what is green stays green.

I've given away a closetful
of woolens, said goodbye
to the asterisks of snow,

all that beauty of decay,
the letting go
of yesterday in the leaves,

for a sun-drenched shoreline
and twenty varieties of palm.
And yet I miss

the mood swings of seasons,
the rise and fall
of mercury in my veins.

Driving to Key West

Their scarlet crowns bursting, poincianas
shook shade along our sunlit route.

We followed an arc between the turquoise
ocean and the turquoise bay.

As we rode, linking keys, my cousin talked
about her childhood trip from the coal mines

of Pennsylvania to NYC. She had stayed
with my parents. We could go deep-

sea fishing or scuba diving, signs announced,
but we were just out for a ride.

We ate key lime pie on Duval Street
where tourists off the cruise ships

jammed the shops. She spoke of my mother's
kindness, how she had met

every need and want with a loving hand.
I thought of Mother's face pinched red

with rage, my head stitched like a rag doll.
Some memories, she said, *you don't forget.*

Stillness and Patience

Again this morning
at the yard's edge,
out of a blue nowhere
the heron appears,

flicking feathers,
spraying sunlight,
tucking wings and head
into a soft egg.

When the river is ready,
a foot or so high,
and the mud beneath
busy with movement,

she flounces down
as if to root. Stillness,
she knows, is the secret.
Stillness and patience.

She listens to her eye,
lifting one leg-stick,
then another,
so slowly her body

seems to float in place.
A dark sister, her reflection
in the tannin-stained river
rides beside her as

now! and now! she strikes,
skewering desire.

Mockingbird

I could have sworn
she was following me,
igniting the fire bush,
trembling fronds.

Field guide in hand,
I was learning names
of palms in a state
I was trying to call home:

ponytail, fishtail, foxtail,
old man, teddy bear,
Chinese fan...
Everything is known

by something else.
She stores a songbook
in her throat
written by birds, insects, frogs.

You can become anything,
she seemed to say,
flashing white flags
along an unfamiliar route.

Banyan Roots

From tall limbs
they sway in wind
like a woman
bent on sweeping
the ground
with her wild hair.

They reach.
They reach down
the way dreams
by day
long
for darkness.

They dig.
They dig deep.
They fatten.

Entwined,
they prop
a banyan's weight,
its myriad
green hearts,
on their shoulders.

For a hundred years
they grow stories
high, wide
as a village
where
beneath shade
news gathers.

Garbage

When I lifted
the trash can's lid,
dropping my bag
of used cat litter
and fuzzy fruit—
small as a finger,
a homely lizard
trapped at the bottom
of his world
looked back.

Three days later,
the lid left opened
to moody weather,
he stared up,
a sickly swimmer
in a polluted river,
scaling archipelagoes
of plastic.

At day's end, I thought,
aren't we all garbage?

I tipped the heavy can
onto its side.
OUTOUTOUT
he came,
a green bullet
onto the heaven
of wet grass.

The Mockingbirds' Chase

Was there a nest nearby?
Man and wife teamed up,
their bountiful script
reduced to one song—
Cheet! Cheet!

Black and white,
as no truths are, the tom
slunk under drippy bushes,
skittered the pavement
as the pair screeched,
stabbing the air in chase,
their striped wings
rising-falling,
opening-closing
like flags snagged
in the wind's mouth.

What was threatened,
what needed to be protected
from instinct or appetite
I never knew. Afraid
for the intruder, afraid
for what had been hatched
in troubled hearts,
I went inside.

Blackbirds

Like loosely stitched
  scraps of cloth
    the wind shakes,
       they sweep the sky,
    swarming and swirling
         this way,
     that way,
then drop down
  to blacken a field,
    to crown a tree,
or facing into the wind
      on telephone wires,
        to line up
like musical notes in the same key,
  as if to instruct us
    on the interconnectedness
      of all things.

VI

Never Will Come Again

Never will come again
wishing on the head of a dandelion
when home was a safe place
in the spring that promises everything.

Never will come again
keeping vows lovers make
when the red-throated hummingbird
hovers over bluebells in the summer.

Never will come again
the mind that knows its way
when forests flame
and birdcall pulls south in the fall.

Never will come again
my daughter, lying still where snow
piles up to hide her name
in the bitter months of winter.

In Extremis

*...the taste of it is so full of memories it encompasses
the whole history of losses.* —Stanley Kunitz

Imagine a well of sorrows
deep as your history.
Start the winch turning;
bucket begets bucket.
The scream, say,
of a metal grill
wedding itself
to a tree
brings up
your father's belt
slapping like a beached
eel in a trawl.
In the no-order
of remembering,
your five-year-old fingers
caught in a car door
might succeed
the jellyfish
of your mother's
lopped-off breast
or your sister's
sin of silence.
There's no
associative ring
to the sequence.
A hangnail
might snag
a dead dog;
a simple lyric,
love's bankruptcy.
As if present and past
weren't enough,
whatever dread thing
hasn't happened
imagination fills in.

In Good Company

From Hemingway to Plath, I wasn't shocked
to learn they'd lain on a gurney, drugged so that
their muscles relaxed as their brains convulsed.
Given her magnetism, Judy Garland's treatments,
I imagine, were like an intersection of lightning bolts.
I wonder what Connie Francis and Tammy Wynette
were thinking when the IV stung like liquid fire
before the world collapsed. After he was zapped,
was Ken Kesey limp as sorrow's handkerchief? Did
Cole Porter stop writing lyrics? When he went home,
was life just a little more flat for Dick Cavett?
And what about the insidious tears in my memory,
that ragman on the corner of yesterday.

On the Corner of Yesterday

On the corner of yesterday
a young woman stood
waiting for her bus.

She knew she was going
somewhere important.
Her mother's hand

kept pushing her forward.
Whacked out of childhood
with her daddy's belt, she grew

hips and breasts, weapons
to overcome the enemy.
Now she would keep her body

aimed straight ahead.
There were dreams
open as savannahs.

Wisdom, Love, Beauty,
shadows on Plato's cave wall,
lined up like promises.

She was patient. She would
wait for as long as it took
for her bus to arrive.

The Return

When the egret returned to the cove in March
she took it as a sign. How it kept walking
out of itself and emerging whole from its hunger.
It was a clear morning, the cherry tree shaking
into bloom over the tannin-stained river.
All winter she had been stuck as if at the bottom
of an abyss waiting for spring rain to pool
and float her up. Now this: the sun pouring in
and the waking wind; the egret pulling
the legs of the tide into her back yard
where the cherry tree bends to admire itself.
These were ladder rungs. So she climbed.
And the egret tucked the S of its neck
to its breast, unfolded its white wings
like an offering of good news, and lifted
into a gold-spattered, infinite blue.

The Undressing Room

Like a zipper that opens its teeth
slowly to ungirdle flesh,
she let out a long sigh.
Stepping out of posture and pose
had come easy:
confident smile, erect stance,
the hand that shook the world
firmly in greeting.
As she looked in the mirror,
what lay beneath made her gasp.
Like a nesting doll
locked too long in the dark,
a wild-eyed girl glared back.
This isn't me, can't be me.
Shaking doubt from her shoes,
fear from her fists,
expletives from her tongue,
she couldn't undress
fast enough. She peeled away
the thousand layers
of unlovable
and not-good-enough
until the mirror
exposed a younger image.
Mothering herself,
she helped the child undress.
She took off the scratchy wool
of *no!* and *don't!*
She removed the pinched expectations
of *must!* and *should!*
She unbuttoned the eyes,
unplugged the mouth.
Letting toes and fingers wiggle,
the body felt again
its nakedness.
But an undressing room
can be a raw place

of forgetfulness,
and so she wrapped
the beginning of herself
in *yes* and *good* and *blessed.*

Purple

All summer, the strung-out
morning glories. The sweet breath
of lilacs in the rain.
Before it turns yellow-brown,
a bruise. A kid's tongue
after a grape Popsicle.
Cotton candy. Cough syrup.
The head of a penis
when it's feeling happy.
Uncooked liver.
The intricate roadmaps
of varicose veins.
Heal-alls by the wayside.
Bathroom walls and florist trucks.
Violet-scented sachets.
Odes. Some prose.
Birthmarks. Hematomas.
Barbie's sports car.
The supple leather
of polished eggplants.
Mogen David wine.
Appassionatas. Most sonatas.
Bridesmaid gowns.
Scented stationery.
Easter eggs and Easter hats.
Barney's skin. In moonlight
the shimmer along a bat's wings.
Lace-trimmed
French underwear. Choir robes.
Black cherry ice cream.
If it looks back over its shoulder
as it slips below the horizon,
the last color the sun sees.

Woman in Blue

After Jackie *by Rachel Gecan-Rondinelli Lapinski*

Framed in the doorway,
she could be any
wife waiting
for a husband
to arrive and start
the clock moving.
But there's nothing
in the oven, the table
is empty, and there is
no husband. Dressed
in the blue of twilight,
she could be waiting
for her life to arrive
as it might in a dream
or a song floating in
on the wind's back.
But she's waiting
on nobody.
She's waiting
for nothing.
Content to stand
in the anteroom
of action, she lets go
of the day's worries
and eases into
the cool
erasure of evening.

Dusk

Now it is time to leave
lists and promises behind,
to sit on the porch and watch
the moon float like a white dish

on gray water as stars begin
to pixilate the sky.
Listen to evening song,
crickets tuning their strings

in the tall grass, the flapping
of bat wings. A blue heron
on the lake's rim disappears.
Trees merge with their shadows.

Now it is time to lay down
the day's cares. Forgive yourself.
The judging eye of the sun
gives way to twilight and twilight

dissolves misspoken words
and deeds not done. Now the wind
carries your name to the treetops
as night comes in its black robe.

The Corridor

After Eerie Lane *by Siegfried Zademack*

There's a candle-lit corridor I walk
each night in dreams. Shadows
fall across my path as I step forward
on a walkway moving backwards.

The candles wear haloes, reflecting
on the opposite wall as ghosts
of themselves. Like the Jews' miracle
of the oil, for as long as I walk

they stay lit. The blue rectangle
at the end of the corridor is not
a blazing light. It is an emptiness
that can't be filled. Yet

its pull is irresistible as breath.
Night after night I aim myself
straight at infinity and wear out
my shoes walking.

Vows for the New Year

I will ride the day to new places,
reclaiming my child's wonder:
a buttercup's reflected face,

the fallen star of a lightning bug,
the baton of a happy dog's tail.
I will smile easily and often, hug

the shoulders of each passing second
knowing it will not come again.
I will cultivate deserts, bend

sunlight to glister off sad highways.
I will make food my friend, not my lover.
I will walk three miles every day

and greet my neighbors. At sixty-eight
I will honor the body's complaints,
forgive mirrors their honesty.

I will wear gratitude like a red coat,
forbearing the shifting
seasons of hope and doubt.

Acknowledgments

I am grateful to the editors of the journals in which these poems first appeared, some in different forms.

Calliope: "The Red Kayak"
Chaffey Review: "Purple," "A Reminder to Myself of What I Love"
First Literary Review: "A Brief Existential Rumination"
FutureCycle Poetry: "Woman in ICU," "Vows for the New Year"
Goodreads Newsletter: "Le dejeuner sur l'herbe," "The Death of the
     Poet Li Po," "Sergei Aleksandrovitch Esenin's Last Poem"
Her/Mark: "The Return," "The Imagined Man"
Innisfree: "Winter Storm"
IthacaLit: "Dolor of the Abandoned House," "After *The Loss
     of Virginity*"
Jewish Woman's Literary Annual: "What Else But Love," "Hiking
     Brokenback Mountain"
Lighthouse Point Magazine: "The Millionaire," "How to Start
     a Day," "Dusk"
Nimrod International Journal: "In Extremis"
Persimmon Tree: "Tour Guide in the Musée du Louvres"
Poetry Society of Virginia Newsletter: "Japanese Cherry Blossom"
Ripasso: "The Long Life"
River Oak Review: "Contemplating *Lovers in the Red Sky*"
Skipping Stones: "Past Midnight"
Vilna Review: "Grandma Mamie's Kitchen"

The following poems won first place awards in the annual contest sponsored by the Poetry Society of Virginia:

2007: "The Return," "The Undressing Room"
2009: "Tour Guide in the Musée du Louvres," "What His Gift of
     Flowers Said"
2012: "Sergei Aleksandrovitch Esenin's Last Poem," "Grandpa's
     Tulips," "Dance Lessons"

"Woman in Blue" was featured in *Merge: Ekphrastic Poetry & Art Show,* Olde Towne Art Gallery, Portsmouth, Virginia, in February 2012.

"The Egret," "After Moving from Virginia to Florida," and "Driving to Key West" were formally displayed in libraries in Broward County, Florida, in April 2011 in "The All About Broward Poetry Project" produced by Anastasia Clark.

"Earhart's Last Poem" was included in the album "Our Poetic Tribute to Amelia Earhart," also produced by Anastasia Clark, which is housed in the Amelia Earhart Birthplace Museum in Kansas and copies distributed to libraries throughout Broward County, Florida.

I am indebted to the members of the Fort Lauderdale Writers' Group for their support; for their wise editorial suggestions, my sisters in poetry Mary McCue, Mary-Jean Kledzik, and my beloved daughter Hara Glasser-Frei.

Cover art, "The Red Coat," by Fontini Hamidieli (www.veriart.gr); author photo by Kia Ewing; cover and interior book design by Diane Kistner (dkistner@futurecycle.org); Gentium Book text with Helvetica Neue titling

About FutureCycle Press

FutureCycle Press is dedicated to publishing lasting English-language poetry and flash fiction books, chapbooks, and anthologies in both print-on-demand and ebook formats. Founded in 2007 by long-time independent editor/publishers and partners Diane Kistner and Robert S. King, the press incorporated as a nonprofit in 2012.
A number of our editors are distinguished poets and authors in their own right, and we have been actively involved in the small press movement going back to the early seventies.

The FutureCycle Poetry Book Prize and honorarium is awarded annually for the best full-length volume of poetry we publish in a calendar year. We are dedicated to giving all authors we publish the care their work deserves, making our catalog of titles the most distinguished it can be, and paying forward any earnings to fund more great books.

We've learned a few things about independent publishing over the years. We've also evolved a unique, resilient publishing model that allows us to focus mainly on vetting and preserving for posterity the most books of exceptional quality without becoming overwhelmed with bookkeeping and mailing, fundraising activities, or taxing editorial and production "bubbles." To find out more about what we are doing, come see us at www.futurecycle.org.

The FutureCycle Poetry Book Prize

All full-length volumes of poetry published by FutureCycle Press in a given calendar year are considered for the annual FutureCycle Poetry Book Prize. This allows us to consider each submission on its own merits, outside of the context of a contest. Too, the judges see the finished book, which will have benefitted from the beautiful book design and strong editorial gloss we are famous for.

The book ranked the best in judging will be announced as the prize-winner in the subsequent year. There is no fixed monetary award; instead, the winning poet will receive an honorarium of 20% of our total net royalties from all poetry books and chapbooks we sold online that year. (For example, in 2013, the winner of the 2012 book prize was announced and received a cash award from the 2012 royalties.) The winner is also accorded the honor of judging the next year's competition.

16780277R00051

Made in the USA
Charleston, SC
10 January 2013